Hannah More

Percy, a tragedy. As it is acted at the Theatre-Royal in Covent-Garden

Hannah More

Percy, a tragedy. As it is acted at the Theatre-Royal in Covent-Garden

ISBN/EAN: 9783741164910

Manufactured in Europe, USA, Canada, Australia, Japa

Cover: Foto ©Andreas Hilbeck / pixelio.de

Manufactured and distributed by brebook publishing software (www.brebook.com)

Hannah More

Percy, a tragedy. As it is acted at the Theatre-Royal in Covent-Garden

PERCY,

A

TRAGEDY.

AS IT IS ACTED AT THE

THEATRE-ROYAL

IN

COVENT-GARDEN.

The FOURTH EDITION.

LONDON:
Printed for T. CADELL, in the Strand.
M DCC LXXXVIII.

[Price ONE SHILLING and SIXPENCE.]

TO

EARL PERCY:

This TRAGEDY,

AS

A SMALL TRIBUTE

To His Illustrious CHARACTER,

IS

VERY RESPECTFULLY

INSCRIB'D:

By His Lordship's

Most obedient,

AND

Most humble Servant,

HANNAH MORE.

Dramatis Personæ.

M E N.

PERCY, } Earl of Northumberland. { Mr. Lewis.

EARL DOUGLAS,   Mr. Wroughton.

EARL RABY, *Elwina's Father*, Mr. Aikin.

EDRIC, *Friend to Douglas*, Mr. Whitfield.

HARCOURT, *Friend to Percy*, Mr. Robson.

SIR HUBERT, *a Knight*, Mr. Hull.

W O M E N.

ELWINA,   Mrs. Barry.

BIRTHA,   Mrs. Jackson.

KNIGHTS, GUARDS, ATTENDANTS, &c.

SCENE, *Raby Castle, in Durham.*

PROLOGUE.

Written by Mr. GARRICK.

Spoken by Mrs. BULKELY.

THO' I'm a female, and the rule is ever,
For us, in Epilogue, to beg your favour,
Yet now I take the lead—and, leaving art
And envy to the men—with a warm heart,
A woman here I come—to take a woman's part.
No little jealousies my mind perplex,
I come, the friend and champion of my sex;
I'll prove, ye fair, that let us have our swing,
We can, as well as men, do any thing;
Nay, better too, perhaps—for now and then,
These times produce some bungling among men,
In spite of lordly wits—with force and ease,
Can't we write plays, or damn 'em, if we please?
The men, who grant not much, allow us charms—
Are eyes, shapes, dimples, then, our only arms?
To rule this man our sex dame Nature teaches;
Mount the high horse we can, and make long speeches;
Nay, and with dignity, some wear the breeches;
And why not wear 'em?—We shall have your votes,
While some of t' other sex wear petticoats.
Did not a Lady Knight, late Chevalier,
A brave, smart soldier to your eyes appear?
Hey! presto! pass! his sword becomes a fan,
A comely woman rising from the man.

PROLOGUE

The French their Amazonian maid invite—
She goes—alike well skill'd to talk or write,
Dance, ride, negociate, scold, coqet, or fight.
If she should set her heart upon a rover,
And he prove false, she'd kick her faithless lover.
The Greeks and Romans own our boundless claim—
The Muses, Graces, Virtues, Fortune, Fame,
Wisdom and Nature too, they women call;
With this sweet flatt'ry—yet they mix some gall—
'Twill out—the Furies too are females all.
The pow'rs of Riches, Physic, War, and Wine,
Sleep, Death, and Devils too—are masculine.
Are we unfit to rule?—a poor suggestion!
Austria and Russia answer well that question.
If joy from sense and matchless grace arise,
With your own treasure, Britons, bless your eyes:
If such there are—sure, in an humbler way,
The sex, without much guilt, may write a play:
That they've done nobler things, there's no denial;
With all your judgment, then, prepare for trial—
Summon your critic pow'rs, your manhood summon,
A brave man will protect, not hurt a woman;
Let us wish modestly to share with men,
If not the force, the feather of the pen.

EPI-

EPILOGUE.

Written by Mr. GARRICK.

Spoken by Mr. LEE LEWES.

I Must, will speak—I hope my dress and air
   Announce the man of fashion, and no player;
Tho' gentlemen are now forbid the scenes,
Yet have I rush'd thro' heroes, kings, and queens;
Resolv'd, in pit to this polish'd age,
To drive these ballad-heroes from the stage—
   " To drive the deer with hound and horn,
    " Earl Percy took his way;
   " The child may rue, that is unborn,
    " The hunting of that day."
A pretty basis, truly, for a modern play!
What! shall a scribbling, senseless woman dare
To your refinements offer such coarse fare?
Is Douglas, or is Percy, fir'd with passion,
Ready for love or glory, death to dash on,
Fit company for modern still-life men of fashion?
Such madness will our hearts but slightly graze,
We've no such frantic nobles now a-days.
Heart-strings, like fiddle-strings, vibrate no tone,
Unless they're tun'd in perfect unison;
And youths of yore, with ours can ne'er agree—
They're in too sharp, ours in too flat a key.
Could we be'ieve old stories, those strange fellows
Married for love—could of their wives be jealous—

                              Nay,

EPILOGUE.

Nay, conſtant to 'em too—and, what is worſe,
The vulgar ſouls thought cuckoldom a curſe.
Moſt wedded pairs had then one purſe, one mind,
One bed too—ſo prepoſterouſly kind—
From ſuch barbarity (thank heav'n) we're much reſin'd.

Old ſongs their happineſs at home record,
From home they ſep'rate carriages abhorr'd—
One horſe ſerv'd both—my lady rode behind my lord.
'Twas death alone could ſnap their bonds aſunder—
Now tack'd ſo ſlightly, not to ſnap's the wonder.
Nay, death itſelf could not their hearts divide,
They mix'd their love with monumental pride,
For, cut in ſtone, they ſtill lie ſide by ſide.
But why theſe gothic anceſtors produce?
Why ſcour their ruſty armours? What's the uſe?
'Twould not your nicer optics much regale,
To ſee us beaux bend under coats of mail;
Should we our limbs with iron doublets bruiſe,
Good heav'n! how much court-plaiſter we ſhould uſe:
We wear no armour now—but on our ſhoes.
Let not with barbariſm true taſte be blended;
Old vulgar virtues cannot be defended,
Let the dead reſt—we living can't be mended.

ADVERTISEMENT.

The French Drama, founded on the famous old Story of Raoul de Coucy, ſuggeſted to the Author ſome Circumſtances in the former part of this Tragedy.

PERCY,

A TRAGEDY.

ACT I.

SCENE, *A Gothic Hall.*

Enter EDRIC *and* BIRTHA.

BIRTHA.

WHAT may this mean? Earl Douglas has injoin'd thee
To meet him here in private?

EDRIC.

Yes, my sister,
And this injunction I have oft receiv'd;
But when he comes, big with some painful secret,
He starts, looks wild, then drops ambiguous hints,
Frowns, hesitates, turns pale, and says 'twas nothing;
Then feigns to smile, and by his anxious care
To prove himself at ease, betrays his pain.

B   BIRTHA.

PERCY.

BIRTHA.

Since my short sojourn here, I've mark'd this Earl,
And tho' the ties of blood unite us closely,
I shudder at his haughtiness of temper,
Which not his gentle wife, the bright Elwina,
Can charm to rest. Ill are their spirits pair'd,
His is the seat of frenzy, her's of softness,
His love is transport, her's, is trembling duty,
Rage in his soul is as the whirlwind fierce,
While her's ne'er felt the pow'r of that rude passion.

EDRIC.

Perhaps the mighty soul of Douglas mourns,
Because inglorious love detains him here,
While our bold knights, beneath the Christian
   standard,
Press to the bulwarks of Jerusalem.

BIRTHA.

Tho' every various charm adorns Elwina,
And tho' the noble Douglas doats to madness,
Yet some dark mystery involves their fate:
The canker grief devours Elwina's bloom,
And on her brow meek resignation sits,
Hopeless, yet uncomplaining.

EDRIC.

'Tis most strange.

BIRTHA.

Once, not long since, she thought herself alone;
'Twas then the pent-up anguish burst its bounds;
With broken voice, clasped hands, and streaming
   eyes,
She call'd upon her father, call'd him cruel,
And said her duty claim'd far other recompence.

EDRIC.

EDRIC.

Perhaps the abſence of the good Lord Raby,
Who, at her nuptials, quitted this fair caſtle,
Reſigning it to her, may thus afflict her.
Haſt thou e'er queſtion'd her, good Birtha?

BIRTHA.

                    Often;
But hitherto in vain, and yet ſhe ſhews me
Th' endearing kindneſs of a ſiſter's love;
But if I ſpeak of Douglas——

EDRIC.

                    See! he comes.
It would offend him ſhou'd he find you here.

Enter DOUGLAS.

How! Edric and his ſiſter in cloſe conference?
Do they not ſeem alarm'd at my approach?
And ſee, how ſuddenly they part! Now, Edric,
                    [*Exit Birtha.*
Was this well done? or was it like a friend,
When I deſir'd to meet thee here alone,
With all the warmth of truſting confidence,
To lay my boſom naked to thy view,
And ſhew thee all its weakneſs, was it well
To call thy ſiſter here, to let her witneſs
Thy friend's infirmity?—perhaps to tell her——

EDRIC.

My lord, I nothing know; I came to learn.

DOUGLAS.

Nay then thou doſt ſuſpect there's ſomething
          wrong!

EDRIC.

EDRIC.

If we were bred from infancy together,
If I partook in all thy youthful griefs,
And every joy thou knew'st was doubly mine;
Then tell me all the secret of thy soul:
" Or have these few short months of separation,
" The only absence we have ever known,
" Have these so rent the bands of love asunder,
" That Douglas should distrust his Edric's truth?

DOUGLAS.

My friend, I know thee faithful as thou'rt brave
And I will trust thee—but not now, good Edric,
'Tis past, 'tis gone, it is not worth the telling,
'Twas wrong to cherish what disturb'd my peace;
I'll think of it no more.

EDRIC.

    Transporting news!
I fear'd some hidden trouble vex'd your quiet.
In secret I have watch'd——

DOUGLAS.

    Ha! watch'd in secret?
A spy? employ'd, perhaps, to note my actions?
What have I said? Forgive me, thou art noble:
Yet do not press me to disclose my grief,
For when thou know'st it, I perhaps shall hate
  thee
As much, my Edric, as I hate myself
For my suspicions, I am ill at ease.

EDRIC.

How will the fair Elwina grieve to hear it!

DOUGLAS.

Hold, Edric, hold—thou haft touch'd the fatal
    string
That wakes me into madness. Hear me then,
But let the deadly secret be secur'd
With bars of adamant in thy close breast.
Think on the curse which waits on broken oaths;
A knight is bound by more than vulgar ties,
And perjury in thee were doubly damn'd,
Well then, the king of England—

EDRIC.
                  Is expected
From distant Palestine.

DOUGLAS.
             Forbid it, heaven,
For with him comes—

EDRIC.
           Ah! who?

DOUGLAS.
            Peace, peace,
For see Elwina's here. Retire, my Edric;
When next we meet thou shalt know all. Farewel.
                              [Exit Edric.
Now to conceal with care my bosom's anguish,
And let her beauty chase away my sorrows!
Yes, I wou'd meet her with a face of smiles—
But 'twill not be.

                                        Enter

Enter ELWINA.

ELWINA.
    Alas, 'tis ever thus!
Thus ever clouded is his angry brow.   *(Aside.*

DOUGLAS.
I were too bleft, Elwina, cou'd I hope
You met me here by choice, or that your bosom
Shar'd the warm transports mine must ever feel
At your approach.

ELWINA.
    My lord, if I intrude,
The cause which brings me claims at least for-
  givenefs:
I fear you are not well, and come, unbidden,
Except by faithful duty, to enquire,
If haply in my power, my little power,
I have the means to minister relief
To your affliction?

DOUGLAS.
    What unwonted goodness!
O I were bleft above the lot of man,
If tendernefs, not duty, brought Elwina;
Cold, ceremonious, and unfeeling duty,
That wretched fubstitute for love: But know,
The heart demands a heart; nor will be paid
With lefs than what it gives. E'en now, Elwina,
The gliftening tear ftands trembling in your eyes
Which caft their mournful fweetnefs on the ground,
As if they fear'd to raife their beams to mine,
And read the language of reproachful love.

ELWINA.

ELWINA.

My lord, I hop'd the thousand daily proofs
Of my obedience——

DOUGLAS.

Death to all my hopes!
Heart rending word! obedience? what's obe-
  dience?
'Tis fear, 'tis hate, 'tis terror, 'tis aversion,
'Tis the cold debt of ostentatious duty,
Paid with insulting caution, to remind me
How much you tremble to offend a tyrant
So terrible as Douglas.—" O Elwina——
" While duty measures the regard it owes,
" With scrupulous precision, and nice justice,
" Love never reasons, but profusely gives,
" Gives like a thoughtless prodigal its all,
" And trembles then, left it has done too little."

ELWINA.

Indeed I'm most unhappy that my cares,
And my solicitude to please, offend.

DOUGLAS.

True tenderness is less solicitous,
Less prudent and more fond; th' enamour'd heart
Conscious it loves; and blest in being lov'd,
Reposes on the object it adores,
And trusts the passion it inspires and feels.—
Thou hast not learnt how terrible it is
To feed a hopeless flame.—But hear, Elwina,
Thou most obdurate, hear me.——

ELWINA:

Say, my lord,
For your own lips shall vindicate my fame,
Since

Since at the altar I became your wife;
Can malice charge me with an act, a word,
I ought to blush at? Have I not still liv'd
As open to the eye of observation,
As fearless innocence shou'd ever live?
I call attesting angels to be witness,
If in my open deed, or secret thought,
My conduct, or my heart, they've ought discern'd
Which did not emulate their purity.

DOUGLAS.

This vindication e'er you were accus'd,
" This warm defence, repelling all attacks
" E'er they are made, and construing casual words
" To formal accusations, trust me, Madam"
Shews rather an alarm'd and vigilant spirit,
For ever on the watch to guard its secret,
Than the sweet calm of fearless innocence.
Who talk'd of guilt? Who testified suspicion?

ELWINA.

Learn, Sir, that virtue, while 'tis free from blame,
Is modest, lowly, meek, and unassuming;
Not apt, like fearful vice, to shield its weakness,
Beneath the studied pomp of boastful phrase,
Which swells to hide the poverty it shelters;
But when this virtue feels itself suspected,
Insulted, set at nought, its whiteness stain'd,
It then grows proud, forgets its humble worth,
And rates itself above its real value.

DOUGLAS.

I did not mean to chide! But think, O think,
What pangs must rend this fearful, doating heart,
To see you sink impatient of the grave,
To feel, distracting thought, to feel you hate me!

ELWINA.

ELWINA.

What if the slender thread by which I hold
This poor precarious being soon must break;
Is it Elwina's crime, or heav'n's decree?
Yet I shall meet, I trust, the king of terrors,
Submissive and resign'd, without one pang,
One fond regret at leaving this gay world.

DOUGLAS.

Yes, Madam, there is one, one man ador'd,
For whom your sighs will heave, your tears will
    flow,
For whom this hated world will still be dear,
For whom you still wou'd live——

ELWINA.

              Hold, hold, my lord,
What may this mean?

DOUGLAS.

              Ah! I have gone too far.
What have I said?———Your father, sure, your
    father,
The good Lord Raby may at least expect
One tender sigh.

ELWINA.

              Alas, my lord, I thought
The precious incense of a daughter's sighs
Might rise to heav'n, and not offend its ruler.

DOUGLAS.

'Tis true; yet Raby is no more belov'd
Since he bestow'd his daughter's hand on Douglas:
That was a crime the dutiful Elwina

Can never pardon; and believe me, Madam,
My love's so nice, so delicate my honour,
I am asham'd to owe my happiness
To ties which make you wretched. [*Exit Douglas.*

ELWINA.

Ah! how's this?
Tho' I have ever found him fierce and rash,
Full of obscure surmises, and dark hints,
Till now he never ventur'd to accuse me.
Yet there is one, one man belov'd, ador'd,
For whom your tears will flow—these were his
    words—
And then the wretched subterfuge of Raby—
How poor th' evasion!—But my Birtha comes.

Enter BIRTHA.

BIRTHA.

Crossing the Portico I met Lord Douglas,
Disorder'd were his looks, his eyes shot fire;
He call'd upon your name with such distraction,
I fear'd some sudden evil had befall'n you.

ELWINA.

Not sudden; no, long has the storm been ga-
    thering,
Which threatens speedily to burst in ruin,
On this devoted head.

BIRTHA.

I ne'er beheld
Your gentle soul so ruffled, yet I've mark'd you,
While others thought you happiest of the happy,
Blest with whate'er the world calls great, or good,
                                                With

With all that nature, all that fortune gives,
I've mark'd you bending with a weight of sorrow.

ELWINA.

O I will tell thee all! thou cou'dst not find
An hour, a moment in Elwina's life,
When her full heart so long'd to ease its burthen,
And pour its sorrows in thy friendly bosom;
Hear then with pity, hear my tale of woe.
And, O forgive, kind nature, filial piety,
If my presumptuous lips arraign a father!
Yes, Birtha, that belov'd, that cruel father,
Has doom'd me to a life of hopeless anguish,
To die of grief e'er half my days are number'd,
Doom'd me to give my trembling hand to Douglas,
'Twas all I had to give, my heart was—Percy's.

BIRTHA.
What do I hear?

ELWINA.
My mis'ry, not my crime.
Long since the battle 'twixt the rival houses,
Of Douglas and of Percy, for whose hate
This mighty globe's too small a Theatre,
One summer's morn my father chas'd the Deer,
On Cheviot Hills, Northumbria's fair domain.—

BIRTHA.
On that fam'd spot where first the feuds commenc'd
Between the Earls?

C 2   ELWINA.

ELWINA.

The same. During the chace,
Some of my father's knights receiv'd an insult
From the Lord Percy's herdsmen, churlish foresters,
Unworthy of the gentle blood they serv'd,
My father, proud and jealous of his honour,
(Thou know'st the fiery temper of our Barons)
Swore that Northumberland had been concern'd
In this rude outrage, nor wou'd hear of peace,
Or reconcilement which the Percy offer'd;
But bade me hate, renounce, and banish him.
O! 'twas a task too hard for all my duty,
I strove, and wept, I strove—but still I lov'd.

BIRTHA.

Indeed 'twas most unjust; but say what follow'd?

ELWINA.

Why shou'd I dwell on the disastrous tale?
Forbid to see me, Percy soon embark'd,
With our great king against the Saracen.
Soon as the jarring kingdoms were at peace,
Earl Douglas, whom till then I ne'er had seen,
Came to this castle; 'twas my hapless fate
To please him.—Birtha! thou can'st tell what
    follow'd:
But who shall tell the agonies I felt?
My barbarous father forc'd me to dissolve
The tender vows himself had bid me form——
He dragg'd me trembling, dying, to the altar,
I sigh'd, I struggled, fainted, and complied.

BIRTHA.

Did Douglas know a marriage had been once
Propos'd 'twixt you and Percy?

EL-

Elwina.

If he did,
He thought, like you, it was a match of policy,
Nor knew our love surpass'd our father's prudence.

Birtha.

Should he now find he was the instrument
Of the Lord Raby's vengeance?

Elwina.

'Twere most dreadful!
My father lock'd this motive in his breast,
And feign'd to have forgot the Chace of Cheviot.
Some moons have now completed their slow course
Since my sad marriage.—Percy still is absent.

Birtha.

Nor will return before his sov'reign comes.

Elwina.

Talk not of his return! this coward heart
Can know no thought of peace but in his absence.
How, Douglas here again? some fresh alarm!

Enter Douglas, *agitated, with letters in his hand.*

Douglas.

Madam, your pardon——

ELWINA.
What disturbs my lord?

DOUGLAS.
Nothing.—Disturb? I ne'er was more at ease.
These letters from your father give us notice
He will be here to-night;—He further adds
The king's each hour expected.

ELWINA.
How? the King?
Said you the king?

DOUGLAS.
And 'tis Lord Raby's pleasure
That you among the foremost bid him welcome,
You must attend the court.

ELWINA.
Must I, my lord?

DOUGLAS.
Now to observe how she receives the news!
(Aside.

ELWINA.
I must not,—cannot.—By the tender love
You have so oft profess'd for poor Elwina,
Indulge this one request—O let me stay!

DOUGLAS.
Enchanting sounds! she does not wish to go—
(Aside.

EL-

ELWINA.

The buſtling world, the pomp which waits on
  greatneſs,
Ill ſuits my humble, unambitious ſoul;—
Then leave me here, to tread the ſafer path
Of private life, here, where my peaceful courſe
Shall be as ſilent as the ſhades around me;
Nor ſhall one vagrant wiſh be e'er allow'd
To ſtay beyond the bounds of Raby Caſtle.

DOUGLAS.

O muſic to my ears! *(Aſide.)*—Can you reſolve
To hide thoſe wondrous beauties in the ſhade,
Which rival kings wou'd cheaply buy with empire?
Can you renounce the pleaſures of a court,
Whoſe roofs reſound with minſtrelſy and mirth?

ELWINA.

My lord, retirement is a wife's beſt duty,
And virtue's ſafeſt ſtation is retreat.

DOUGLAS.

My ſoul's in tranſports! *(Aſide.)*—But can you
  forego
What wins the ſoul of woman—admiration?
A world, where charms inferior far to yours,
Only preſume to ſhine when you are abſent?
Will you not long to meet the public gaze?
Long to eclipſe the fair, and charm the brave?

ELWINA.

Theſe are delights in which the *mind* partakes
  not.

DOUGLAS.

DOUGLAS.

I'll try her farther. *(Aside.)*
(Takes her hand, and looks stedfastly at her as he speaks.)
     But reflect once more;
When you shall hear that England's gallant peers,
Fresh from the fields of war, and gay with glory,
All vain with conquest, and elate with fame,
When you shall hear these princely youths contend,
In many a tournament for beauty's prize;
When you shall hear of revelry, and masking,
Of mimic combats, and of festive halls,
Of lances shiver'd in the cause of love,
Will you not then repent, then wish your fate,
Your happier fate had till that hour reserv'd you
For some plum'd conqueror?

ELWINA.

    My fate, my lord,
Is now bound up with yours.

DOUGLAS.

    Here let me kneel——
Yes, I will kneel, and gaze, and weep, and wonder;
Thou paragon of goodness!—pardon, pardon,
     (Kisses her hand.)
I am convinc'd—I can no longer doubt,
Nor talk, nor hear, nor reason, nor reflect.
—I must retire, and give a loose to joy.
     [*Exit Douglas.*

BIRTHA.

The king returns.

ELWINA.
And with him Percy comes!

BIRTHA.
You needs must go.

ELWINA.
Shall I folicit ruin,
And pull deftruction on me ere its time?
I, who have held it criminal to name him?
I will not go——I difobey thee, Douglas,
But difobey thee to preferve thy honour.

End of the Firſt Act.

ACT II.

SCENE, *The Hall.*

Douglas, speaking as he enters.

SEE that the traytor instantly be seiz'd,
And strictly watch'd: let none have access to him.
 O jealousy, thou aggregate of woes!
Were there no hell, thy torments wou'd create one.
But yet she may be guiltless—may? she must.
How beautiful she look'd! pernicious beauty!
Yet innocent, as bright, seem'd the sweet blush
That mantled on her cheek. But not for me,
But not for me those breathing roses blow!
And then she wept—what! can I bear her tears?
Well—let her weep—her tears are for another;
O did they fall for me, to dry their streams,
I'd drain the choicest blood that feeds this heart,
Nor think the drops I shed were half so precious.
 (He stands in a musing posture.)

Enter Lord RABY.

RABY.

Sure I mistake—Am I in Raby Castle?
Impossible! that was the seat of smiles;
And Cheerfulness, and Joy, were household gods.
 I us'd

PERCY.

I us'd to scatter pleasures when I came,
An! ev'ry servant shar'd his lord's delight.
But now Suspicion and Distrust dwell here,
And Discontent maintains a sullen sway.
Where is the smile unfeign'd, the joyal welcome,
Which cheer'd the sad, beguil'd the pilgrim's pain,
And made dependency forget its bonds?
Where is the ancient, hospitable hall,
Whose vaulted roof once rung with harmless mirth;
Where every passing stranger was a guest,
And every guest a friend. I fear me much,
If once our nobles scorn their rural seats,
Their rural greatness, and their vassals love,
Freedom, and English grandeur, are no more.

DOUGLAS.
(advancing)
My lord, you are welcome.

RABY.
Sir, I trust I am;
But yet, methinks, I shall not feel I'm welcome,
Till my Elwina bleis me with her smiles:
She was not wont with ling'ring step to meet me,
Or greet my coming with a cold embrace;
Now, I extend my longing arms in vain.
My child, my darling, does not come to fill them.
O they were happy days when she wou'd fly
To meet me from the camp, or from the chace,
And with her fondness overpay my toils!
How eager wou'd her tender hands unbrace
The ponderous armour from my war-worn limbs,
And pluck the helmet which oppos'd her kiss!

DOUGLAS.
O sweet delights that never must be mine!

RABY.

RABY.

What do I hear?

DOUGLAS.
Nothing: enquire no farther.

RABY.

My lord, if you respect an old man's peace,
If e'er you doated on my much-lov'd child,
As 'tis most sure you made me think you did,
Then, by the pangs which you may one day feel,
When you, like me, shall be a fond, fond father,
And tremble for the treasure of your age,
Tell me, what this alarming silence means?
You sigh, you do not speak, nay more, you hear not?
Your lab'ring soul turns inward on itself,
As there were nothing but your own sad thoughts
Deserv'd regard. Does my child live?

DOUGLAS.
She does,

RABY.

To bless her father!

DOUGLAS.
And to curse her husband!

RABY.

Ah! have a care, my lord, I'm not so old—

DOUGLAS.

DOUGLAS.

Nor I so base that I should tamely bear it;
Nor am I so inur'd to infamy,
That I can say without a burning blush,
She lives to be my curse.

RABY.

How's this?

DOUGLAS.

I thought
The lily op'ning to the heav'n's soft dews,
Was not so fragrant, and was not so chaste.

RABY.

Has she prov'd otherwise? I'll not believe it.
Who has traduc'd my sweet, my innocent, child?
Yet she's too good to 'scape calumnious tongues.
I know that Slander loves a lofty mark:
It saw her soar a flight above her fellows,
And hurl'd its arrow to her glorious height,
To reach her heart, and bring her to the ground.

DOUGLAS.

Had the rash tongue of Slander so presum'd,
My vengeance had not been of that slow sort,
To need a prompter; nor should any arm,
No, not a father's, dare dispute with mine,
The privilege to die in her defence.
None dares accuse Elwina, but——

RABY.

But who?

DOUGLAS.

DOUGLAS.

But Douglas.

RABY.
(puts his hand to his sword.)

You?—O spare my age's weakness!
You do not know what 'tis to be a father,
You do not know, or you would pity me;
The thousand tender throbs, the nameless feelings,
The dread to ask, and yet the wish to know,
When we adore and fear; but wherefore fear?
Does not the blood of Raby fill her veins?

DOUGLAS.
Percy!—know'st thou that name?

RABY.
How? what of Percy?

DOUGLAS.
He loves Elwina, and my curses on him,
He is belov'd again.

RABY.
I'm on the rack!

DOUGLAS.
Not the two Theban brothers bore each other
Such deep, such deadly hate, as I and Percy.

RABY.
But tell me of my child.

DOUGLAS.

DOUGLAS *(not minding him.)*
            As I and Percy!
When at the marriage rites, O rites accurs'd!
I feiz'd her trembling hand, she started back,
Cold horror thrill'd her veins, her tears flow'd fast.
Fool that I was, I thought 'twas maiden fear,
Dull, doating ignorance! beneath those terrors,
Hatred for me, and love for Percy lurk'd.

RABY.
What proof of guilt is this?

DOUGLAS.
            E'er since our marriage
Our days have still been cold and joyless all;
" Painful restraint, and hatred ill disguis'd,
" Her sole return for all my waste of fondness."
This very morn I told her 'twas your will
She should repair to court; with all those graces,
Which first subdu'd my soul, and still enslave it,
She begg'd to stay behind in Raby Castle,
For courts, and cities had no charms for her.
Curse my blind love! I was again ensnar'd,
And doated on the sweetness which deceiv'd me.
Just at the hour she thought I shou'd be absent,
(For chance cou'd ne'er have tim'd their guilt so
    well,)
Arriv'd young Harcourt, one of Percy's knights,
Strictly enjoin'd to speak to none but her,
I feiz'd the miscreant; hitherto he's silent,
But tortures soon shall force him to confess.

RABY.
Percy is absent—They have never met.
                        DOUG-

DOUGLAS.

At what a feeble hold you grasp for succour!
Will it content me that her person's pure?
No, if her alien heart doats on another,
She is unchaste were not that other Percy.
Let vulgar spirits basely wait for proof,
She loves another—'tis enough for Douglas.

RABY.

Be patient.

DOUGLAS.

Be a tame convenient husband?
And meanly wait for circumstantial guilt?
No—I am nice as the first Cæsar was,
And start at bare suspicion. *(going.)*

RABY *(holding him.)*

Douglas, hear me;
Thou hast nam'd a Roman husband; if she's false,
I mean to prove myself a Roman father.
[Exit Douglas.
This marriage was my work, and thus I'm punish'd!

Enter ELWINA.

ELWINA.

Where is my father? let me fly to meet him,
O let me clasp his venerable knees,
And die of joy in his belov'd embrace.

RABY *(avoiding her embrace.)*
Elwina!

ELWINA.

And is that all? so cold?

RABY.

RABY *(sternly.)*
Elwina!

ELWINA.
Then I'm undone indeed! How stern his looks!
I will not be repuls'd, I am your child,
The child of that dear mother you ador'd;
You shall not throw me off, I will grow here,
And, like the patriarch, wrestle for a blessing.

RABY *(holding her from him.)*
Before I take thee in these aged arms,
Press thee with transport to this beating heart,
And give a loose to all a parent's fondness,
Answer, and see thou answer me as truly
As if the dread enquiry came from heav'n:—
Does no interior sense of guilt confound thee?
Canst thou lay all thy naked soul before me?
Can thy unconscious eye encounter mine?
Canst thou endure the probe, and never shrink?
Can thy firm hand meet mine and never tremble?
Art thou prepar'd to meet the rigid judge?
Or to embrace the fond, the melting father?

ELWINA.
Mysterious heav'n! to what am I reserv'd?

RABY.
Shou'd some rash man, regardless of thy fame,
And in defiance of thy marriage vows,
Presume to plead a guilty passion for thee,
What woud'st thou do?

ELWINA.
What honour bids me do.

E RABY.

RABY.
Come to my arms!   (*they embrace.*

ELWINA.
My father!

RABY.
            Yes, Elwina,
Thou art my child—thy mother's perfect image.

ELWINA.
Forgive these tears of mingled joy and doubt,
For why that question? who should seek to please
The desolate Elwina?

RABY.
            But if any
Should so presume, can'st thou resolve to hate him,
Whate'er his name, whate'er his pride of blood,
Whate'er his former arrogant pretensions?

ELWINA.
Ha!

RABY.
Dost thou falter? Have a care, Elwina.

ELWINA.
Sir, do not fear me; am I not your daughter?

RABY.
Thou hast a higher claim upon thy honour;
Thou art Earl Douglas' Wife.

El-

ELWINA *(weeps.)*
I am indeed!

RABY.
Unhappy Douglas!

ELWINA.
Has he then complain'd?
Has he presum'd to sully my white fame?

RABY.
He knows that Percy——

ELWINA.
Was my destin'd husband;
By your own promise, by a father's promise,
And by a tie more strong, more sacred still,
Mine, by the fast firm bond of mutual love.

RABY.
Now, by my fears, thy husband told me truth.

ELWINA.
If he has told thee that thy only child
Was forc'd, a helpless victim to the altar,
Torn from his arms, who had her virgin heart,
And forc'd to make false vows to one she hated,
Then I confess that he has told thee truth.

RABY.
Her words are barbed arrows in my heart.
But 'tis too late. *(Aside.)* Thou hast appointed
    Harcourt
To see thee here by stealth in Douglas' absence.

Elwina.

No, by my life, nor knew I till this moment
That Harcourt was return'd. Was it for this
I taught my heart to struggle with its feelings?
Was it for this I bore my wrongs in silence?
When the fond ties of early love were broken,
Did my weak soul break out in fond complaints?
Did I reproach thee? Did I call thee cruel?
No—I endur'd it all; and weary'd heaven
To bless the father who destroy'd my peace.

Enter MESSENGER.

Messenger.

My lord, a knight, Sir Hubert as I think,
But newly landed from the holy wars,
Intreats admittance.

Raby.

Let the warrior enter.
[*Exit Messenger.*
All private interests sink at his approach;
All selfish cares be for a moment banish'd!
I've now no child, no kindred but my country.

Elwina.

Weak heart be still, for what hast thou to fear?

Enter Sir HUBERT.

Raby.

Welcome, thou gallant knight, Sir Hubert,
welcome!

Welcome

Welcome to Raby Castle!—In one word,
Is the king safe? Is Palestine subdued?

Sir HUBERT.

The king is safe, and Palestine subdued.

RABY.

Blest be the god of armies! Now, Sir Hubert,
By all the saints thou'rt a right noble knight!
O why was I too old for this crusade?
I think it wou'd have made me young again,
Cou'd I, like thee, have seen the hated Crescent,
Yield to the Christian cross.—How now, Elwina!
What! cold at news which might awake the dead!
If there's a drop in thy degenerate veins
That glows not now, thou art not Raby's daughter.
It is religion's cause, the cause of heav'n!

ELWINA.

When policy assumes religion's name,
And wears the sanctimonious garb of faith,
Only to colour fraud, and licenſe murder,
War then is tenfold guilt.

RABY.

    Blaspheming girl!

ELWINA.

'Tis not the crosier, nor the pontiff's robe,
The saintly look, nor elevated eye,
Nor Palestine destroy'd, nor Jordan's banks
Delug'd with blood of slaughter'd infidels.
No, nor th' extinction of the Eastern world,
Nor all the mad, pernicious, bigot rage

Of

Of your crusades, can bribe that pow'r who sees
The motive with the act. O blind to think
That cruel war can please the prince of peace!
He who erects his altar in the heart,
Abhors the sacrifice of human blood,
And all the false devotion of that zeal,
Which massacres the world he died to save.

RABY.

O impious rage! If thou woud'st shun my curse
No more, I charge thee.———Tell me, good Sir
   Hubert,
Say, have our arms atchiev'd this glorious deed,
(I fear to ask,) without much Christian bloodshed?

ELWINA.

Now heaven support me! *(Aside.)*

Sir HUBERT.

My good lord of Raby,
Imperfect is the sum of human glory!
Wou'd I cou'd tell thee that the field was won,
Without the death of such illustrious knights,
As make the high flush'd cheek of victory pale.

ELWINA.

Why shou'd I tremble thus? *(Aside.)*

RABY.

    Who have we lost?

Sir HUBERT.

The noble Clifford, Walsingham, and Grey,
                      Sir

Sir Harry Hastings, and the valiant Pembroke.
All men of choicest note.

RABY.

     O that my name
Had been enroll'd in such a list of heroes!
If I was too infirm to serve my country,
I might have prov'd my love by dying for her.

ELWINA.
Were there no more?

Sir HUBERT.
    But few of noble blood.
But the brave youth who gain'd the palm of glory,
The flower of knighthood, and the plume of war,
Who bore his banner foremost in the field,
Yet conquer'd more by mercy than the sword,
Was Percy.

ELWINA.
   Then he lives! (*Aside.*)

RABY.
    Did he? Did Percy?
O gallant boy, then I'm thy foe no more;
Who conquers for my country is my friend!
His fame shall add new glories to a house,
Where never maid was false, nor knight disloyal.

Sir HUBERT.
You do embalm him, lady, with your tears:
They grace the grave of glory where he lies,
He died the death of honour.
         EL-

ELWINA.
   Said'ft thou—died?

Sir HUBERT.
Beneath the towers of Solyma he fell.

ELWINA.
      Oh!

Sir HUBERT.
Look to the lady.
   (Elwina faints in her father's arms.

RABY.
      Gentle knight retire——
'Tis an infirmity of nature in her,
She ever mourns at any tale of blood,
She will be well anon—mean time, Sir Hubert,
You'll grace our caftle with your friendly fojourn.

Sir HUBERT.
I muft return with fpeed—health to the lady.
                    [*Exit Hubert.*

RABY.
Look up Elwina. Shou'd her hufband come!
Yet fhe revives not.

Enter DOUGLAS.

DOUGLAS.
   Ha——Elwina fainting?
My lord, I fear you have too harfhly chid her.
                              Her

PERCY.

Her gentle nature could not brook your sternness.
She wakes, she stirs, she feels returning life.
My love!   *(He takes her hand.)*

ELWINA.
O Percy!

DOUGLAS.   *(Starts.)*
Do my senses fail me?

ELWINA.
My Percy, 'tis Elwina calls.

DOUGLAS.
Hell, Hell!

RABY.
Retire awhile, my daughter.

ELWINA.
Douglas here?
My father and my husband!——O for pity?
[Exit Elwina, casting a look of anguish on both.]

DOUGLAS.
Now, now confess she well deserves my ven-
    geance!
Before my face to call upon my foe!

RABY.
Upon a foe who has no power to hurt thee;
Earl Percy's slain.

F   DOUGLAS.

Douglas.

            I live again.—But hold—
Did she not weep? she did, and wept for Percy.
If she laments him, he's my rival still,
And not the grave can bury my resentment.

Raby.

The truly brave are still the truly gen'rous;
Now, Douglas, is the time to prove thee both.
If it be true that she did once love Percy,
Thou hast no more to fear, since he is dead.
Release young Harcourt, let him see Elwina,
'Twill serve a double purpose, 'twill at once
Prove Percy's death, and thy unchang'd affection.
Be gentle to my child, and win her heart,
By confidence, and unreproaching love.

Douglas.

By heav'n thou counsel'st well: it shall be done.
Go get him free, and let him have admittance
To my Elwina's presence.

Raby.

            Farewel, Douglas.
Shew thou believ'st her faithful and she'll prove so.
                      [*Exit Raby.*

Douglas.

Northumberland is dead—that thought is peace!
Her heart may yet be mine, transporting hope!
Percy was gentle, ev'n a foe avows it,
And I'll be milder than a summer's breeze.
Yes, thou most lovely, most ador'd of women,
I'll copy every virtue, every grace,
Of my bless'd rival, happier ev'n in death
To be thus lov'd, than living to be scorn'd.

End of Act the Second.

ACT III.

SCENE, *A Garden at Raby Castle, with a Bower.*

Enter PERCY *and Sir* HUBERT.

Sir HUBERT.

THAT Percy lives, and is return'd in safety,
More joys my soul, than all the mighty conquests
That sun beheld, which rose on Syria's ruin.

PERCY.

I've told thee, good Sir Hubert, by what wonder
I was preserv'd, tho' number'd with the slain.

Sir HUBERT.

'Twas strange indeed!

PERCY.

'Twas heav'n's immediate work!
But let me now indulge a dearer joy,

Talk

Talk of a richer gift of Mercy's hand;
A gift so precious to my doating heart,
That life preserv'd is but a second blessing.
O Hubert, let my soul indulge its softness!
The hour, the spot is sacred to Elwina.
This was her fav'rite walk; I well remember,
(For who forgets that loves as I have lov'd?)
'Twas in that very bower she gave this scarf,
Wrought by the hand of love; she bound it on,
And, smiling, cried, Whate'er befal us, Percy,
Be this the sacred pledge of faith between us.
I knelt, and swore, call'd every pow'r to witness,
No time, no circumstance, shou'd force it from me;
But I wou'd lose my life and that together,
Here I repeat my vow.

Sir Hubert.

               Is this the man
Beneath whose single arm an host was crush'd?
He, at whose name the Saracen turn'd pale?
And when he fell, victorious armies wept,
And mourn'd a conquest they had bought so dear?
How has he chang'd the trumpet's martial note,
And all the stirring clangor of the war,
For the soft melting of the lover's lute!
Why are thine eyes still bent upon the bower?

Percy.

O Hubert, Hubert, to a soul enamour'd,
There is a sort of local sympathy,
Which, when we view the scenes of early passion,
Paints the bright image of the object lov'd,
In stronger colours, than remoter scenes
Cou'd ever paint it, realizes shade,

Dresses

Dresses it up in all the charms it wore,
Talks to it nearer, frames its answers kinder,
Gives form to fancy, and embodies thought.

Sir HUBERT.

I should not be believ'd in Percy's camp,
If I shou'd tell them that their gallant leader,
The thunder of the war, the bold Northumberland,
Renouncing Mars, dissolv'd in amorous wishes,
Loiter'd in shades, and pin'd in rosy bowers,
To catch a transient glance of two bright eyes.

PERCY.

Enough of conquest, and enough of war!
Ambition's cloy'd—the heart resumes its rights.
When England's king, and England's good required,
This arm not idly the keen falchion brandish'd:
Enough—for vaunting misbecomes a soldier.
I live, I am return'd—am near Elwina!
Seest thou those turrets? Yes, that castle holds her.
But wherefore tell thee this? for thou hast seen her.
How look'd, what said she? Did she hear the tale
Of my imagin'd death without emotion?

Sir HUBERT.

Percy, thou hast seen the musk-rose newly blown,
Disclose its bashful beauties to the sun,
Till an unfriendly, chilling storm descended,
Crush'd all its blushing glories in their prime,
Bow'd its fair head, and blasted all its sweetness.
So droop'd the maid, beneath the cruel weight
Of my sad tale.

PERCY.

PERCY.
So tender and so true!

Sir HUBERT.
I left her fainting in her father's arms,
The dying flower yet hanging on the tree.
Ev'n Raby melted at the news I brought,
And envy'd thee thy glory.

PERCY.
Then I am blest!
His hate subdued, I've nothing more to fear.

Sir HUBERT.
My embassy dispatch'd, I left the castle,
Nor spoke to any of Lord Raby's household,
For fear the king should chide the tardiness
Of my return. My joy to find you living,
You have already heard.

PERCY.
But where is Harcourt?
Ere this he shou'd have seen her, told her all,
How I surviv'd, return'd——and how I love!
I tremble at the near approach of bliss,
And scarcely can sustain the joy which waits me.

Sir HUBERT.
Grant heaven the fair-one prove but half so true!

PERCY.
O she is truth itself!

Sir

Sir HUBERT.

     She may be chang'd,
Spite of her tears, her fainting, and alarms.
I know the sex, know them as nature made 'em,
Not such as lovers wish, and poets feign.

PERCY.

To doubt her virtue were suspecting heaven,
'Twere little less than infidelity!
And yet I tremble. Why does terror shake
These firm-strung nerves? But 'twill be ever thus,
When fate prepares us more than mortal bliss,
And gives us only human strength to bear it.

Sir HUBERT.

What beam of brightness breaks thro' yonder
  gloom?

PERCY.

Hubert—she comes! by all my hopes she
  comes!
'Tis she—that blissful vision is Elwina!
But ah! what mean those tears?—She weeps for me!
O transport!—go.—I'll listen unobserved,——
And for a moment taste the precious joy,
The banquet of a tear which falls for love.
      [*Exit Sir Hubert.*
      [*Percy goes into the Bower.*

          Enter

Enter ELWINA.

ELWINA.

Shall I not weep, and have I then no cause?
If I cou'd break th' eternal bands of death,
And wrench the sceptre from his iron grasp;
If I cou'd bid the yawning sepulchre
Restore to life its long committed dust;
If I could teach the slaught'ring hand of war,
To give me back my dear, my murder'd Percy,
Then I indeed might once more cease to weep.

[*Percy comes out of the Bower.*]

PERCY.

Then cease, for Percy lives.

ELWINA.

    Protect me heav'n!

PERCY.

O joy unspeakable! My life! my love!
End of my toils, and crown of all my cares!
Kind as consenting peace, as conquest bright,
Dearer than arms, and lovelier than renown!

ELWINA.

It is his voice—it is, it is my Percy!
And dost thou live?

PERCY.

    I never liv'd till now.

EL-

ELWINA.

And did my sighs, and did my sorrows reach
 thee?
And art thou come at last to dry my tears?
How did'st thou 'scape the fury of the foe?

PERCY.

Thy guardian genius hover'd o'er the field,
And turn'd the hostile spear from Percy's breast,
Lest thy fair image should be wounded there.
But Harcourt should have told thee all my fate,
How I surviv'd——

ELWINA.

Alas! I have not seen him.
Oh! I have suffer'd much.

PERCY.

Of that no more;
For every minute of our future lives,
Shall be so bless'd, that we will learn to wonder,
How we cou'd ever think we were unhappy.

ELWINA.

Percy —I cannot speak.

PERCY.

Those tears how eloquent!
I would not change this motionless, mute joy,
For the sweet strains of angels: I look down
With pity on the rest of human kind,
However great may be their fame of happiness,
And think their niggard fate has giv'n them no-
 thing,

Not giving thee; or granting some small blessing,
Denies them my capacity to feel it.

ELWINA.
Alas! what mean you?

PERCY.
Can I speak my meaning?
'Tis of such magnitude that words would wrong it;
But surely my Elwina's faithful bosom,
Shou'd beat in kind responses of delight,
And feel, but never question what I mean.

ELWINA.
Hold, hold, my heart, thou hast much more to
suffer!

PERCY.
Let the slow form, and tedious ceremony
Wait on the splendid victims of ambition.
Love stays for none of these. Thy father's soften'd,
He will forget the fatal Cheviot Chace;
Raby is brave, and I have serv'd my country;
I wou'd not boast, it was for thee I conquer'd.
Then come, my love.

ELWINA.
O never, never, never.

PERCY.
Am I awake? Is that Elwina's voice?

ELWINA.
Percy, thou most ador'd—and most deceiv'd!
If ever fortitude sustain'd thy soul,

When

When vulgar minds have sunk beneath the stroke,
Let thy imperial spirit now support thee.——
If thou can'st be so wondrous merciful,
Do not, O do not curse me!—but thou wilt,
Thou must—for I have done a fearful deed,
A deed of wild despair, a deed of horror.
I am, I am—

PERCY.
Speak, say, what art thou?

ELWINA.
Married.

PERCY.
Oh!

ELWINA.
Percy, I think I begg'd thee not to curse me;
But now I do revoke the fond petition.
Speak! ease thy bursting soul; reproach, upbraid,
O'erwhelm me with thy wrongs——I'll bear it all.

PERCY.
Open, thou earth, and hide me from her sight!
Did'st thou not bid me curse thee?

ELWINA.
Mercy! mercy!

PERCY.
And have I 'scap'd the Saracen's fell sword,
Only to perish by Elwina's guilt?
I wou'd have bar'd my bosom to the foe,
I wou'd have died, had I but known you wish'd it.

ELWINA.

Percy, I lov'd thee moſt when moſt I wrong'd
    thee;
Yes, by theſe tears I did.

PERCY.

            Married! juſt heav'n!
Married? to whom? Yet wherefore ſhould I know!
It cannot add freſh horrors to thy crime,
Or my deſtruction.

ELWINA.

            Oh! 'twill add to both.
How ſhall I tell? Prepare for ſomething dreadful.
Haſt thou not heard of—Douglas?

PERCY.

            Why 'tis well!
Thou awful power why waſte thy wrath on me?
Why arm omnipotence to cruſh a worm?
I cou'd have fall'n without this waſte of ruin.
Married to Douglas! By my wrongs I like it;
'Tis perfidy compleat, 'tis finiſhed falſehood,
'Tis adding freſh perdition to the ſin,
And filling up the meaſure of offence!

ELWINA.

Oh! 'twas my father's deed; he made his child
An inſtrument of vengeance on thy head.
He wept and threaten'd, ſooth'd me, and com-
        manded.

PERCY.

And you complied, moſt duteouſly complied!

ELWINA.

I cou'd withstand his fury; but his tears,
Ah, they undid me! Percy doſt thou know
The cruel tyranny of tenderneſs?
Haſt thou e'er felt a father's warm embrace?
Haſt thou e'er ſeen a father's flowing tears,
And known that thou cou'dſt wipe thoſe tears away?
If thou haſt felt, and haſt reſiſted theſe,
Then thou may'ſt curſe my weakneſs; but if not,
Thou canſt not pity, for thou canſt not judge.

PERCY.

Let me not hear the muſic of thy voice,
Or I ſhall love thee ſtill, I ſhall forget
Thy fatal marriage, and my ſavage wrongs.

ELWINA.

Doſt thou not hate me, Percy?

PERCY.

Hate thee? Yes,
As dying martyrs hate the righteous cauſe
Of that bleſs'd Power for whom they bleed—I
hate thee.
(They look at each other in ſilent agony.)

Enter HARCOURT.

HARCOURT.

Forgive, my lord, your faithful knight——

PERCY.

Come, Harcourt,
Come and behold the wretch who once was Percy.

HAR-

HARCOURT.

With grief I've learn'd the whole unhappy tale.
Earl Douglas, whose suspicion never sleeps——

PERCY.

What, is the tyrant jealous?

ELWINA.

Hear him, Percy.

PERCY.

I will command my rage—Go on.

HARCOURT.

Earl Douglas
Knew by my arms, and my accoutrements,
That I belong'd to you; he question'd much,
And much he menac'd me, but both alike
In vain, he then arrested and confin'd me.

PERCY.

Arrest my knight? The Scot shall answer it.

ELWINA.

How came you now releas'd?

HARCOURT.

Your noble father
Obtain'd my freedom, having learn'd from Hubert
The news of Percy's death. The good old Lord,
Hearing the king's return, has left the Castle
To do him homage. *To Percy.*
Sir, you had best retire;
Your safety is endanger'd by your stay,
I fear shou'd Douglas know——

PERCY.

PERCY.

Shou'd Douglas know?
Why what new magic's in the name of Douglas,
That it shou'd strike Northumberland with fear?
Go, seek the haughty Scot, and tell him—no—
Conduct me to his presence.

ELWINA.

Percy, hold;
Think not 'tis Douglas—'tis—

PERCY.

I know it well——
Thou mean'st to tell me 'tis Elwina's husband;
But that inflames me to superior madness.
This happy husband, this triumphant Douglas,
Shall not insult my misery with his bliss.
I'll blast the golden promise of his joys.
Conduct me to him—nay, I will have way——
Come let us seek this husband.

ELWINA.

Percy, hear me,
When I was robb'd of all my peace of mind,
My cruel fortune left me still one blessing,
One solitary blessing, to console me;
It was my fame.—'Tis a rich jewel, Percy,
And I must keep it spotless, and unsoil'd:
But thou wou'dst plunder what e'en Douglas
    spar'd,
And rob this single gem of all its brightness.

PERCY.

PERCY.
Go—thou wast born to rule the fate of Percy.
Thou art my conqueror still.

ELWINA.
What noise is that?
(Harcourt goes to the side of the Stage.

PERCY.
Why art thou thus alarm'd?

ELWINA.
Alas! I feel
The cowardice and terrors of the wicked,
Without their sense of guilt.

HARCOURT.
My lord, 'tis Douglas.

ELWINA.
Fly, Percy, and for ever?

PERCY.
Fly from Douglas?

ELWINA.
Then stay, barbarian, and at once destroy
My life and fame.

PERCY.
That thought is death. I go.
My honour to thy dearer honour yields.

ELWINA.
Yet, yet thou art not gone!

PERCY.
   Farewel, farewel!
      [*Exit Percy.*

ELWINA.
I dare not meet the searching eye of Douglas.
I must conceal my terrors.

*Douglas at the Side with his sword drawn, Edric
holds him.*

DOUGLAS.
   Give me way.

EDRIC.
Thou shalt not enter.

DOUGLAS *(struggling with Edric.*
    If there were no hell,
It would defraud my vengeance of its edge,
And he should live.
   (*Breaks from Edric and comes forward.*)
   Curs'd chance! he is not here.

ELWINA. *(going.*
I dare not meet his fury.

DOUGLAS.
    See she flies
With ev'ry mark of guilt—Go, search the Bow'r,
      (*Aside to Edric.*

H   He

He shall not thus escape. Madam, return. *(Aloud.*
Now honest Douglas learn of her to feign. *(Aside.*
Alone, Elwina? who just parted hence?
      (With affected composure.

ELWINA.

My lord, 'twas Harcourt; sure you must have
 met him.

DOUGLAS.

O exquisite dissembler! No one else?

ELWINA.

My lord!

DOUGLAS.

How I enjoy her criminal confusion!
You tremble, Madam.

ELWINA.

    Wherefore shou'd I tremble?
By your permission Harcourt was admitted;
'Twas no mysterious, secret introduction.

DOUGLAS.

And yet you seem alarm'd.—If Harcourt's pre-
 sence
Thus agitates each nerve, makes ev'ry pulse
Thus wildly throb, and the warm tides of blood,
Mount in quick rushing tumults to your cheek;
If friendship can excite such strong emotions,
What tremors had a lover's presence caused?

ELWINA.

Ungenerous man!
        DOUGLAS.

Douglas.

     I feast upon her terrors. (*Aside.*
The story of his death was well contriv'd; *(to her.*
But it affects not me; I have a wife,
Compar'd with whom cold Dian was unchaste.
          (*Takes her hand.*
But mark me well—tho' it concerns not you—
If there's a sin more deeply black than others,
Distinguish'd from the list of common crimes,
A legion in itself, and doubly dear
To the dark prince of hell, it is—hypocrisy.
    (*Throws her from him and Exit.*

Elwina.

Yes, I will bear his fearful indignation!
Thou melting heart be firm as adamant;
Ye shatter'd nerves be strung with manly force,
That I may conquer all my sex's weakness,
Nor let this bleeding bosom lodge one thought,
Cherish one wish, or harbour one desire,
That Angels may not hear, and Douglas know.

End of the Third Act.

ACT

ACT IV.

SCENE, *The Hall.*

Enter DOUGLAS, *his sword drawn and bloody in one hand, in the other a letter.* HARCOURT *wounded.*

DOUGLAS.

TRAYTOR no more. This letter shews thy office.
Twice hast thou robb'd me of my dear revenge.
I took thee for thy leader.—Thy base blood
Wou'd stain the noble temper of my sword,
But as the pander to thy master's lust,
Thou justly fall'st by a wrong'd husband's hand.

HARCOURT.
Thy wife is innocent.

DOUGLAS.
    Take him away.

HARCOURT.
Percy, revenge my fall!
     [*Guards bear Harcourt in.*

Doug-

DOUGLAS.

Now for the letter!
He begs once more to see her,—so 'tis plain
They have already met!—but to the rest——
Reads.
" In vain you wish me to restore the scarf,
Dear pledge of love, while I have life I'll wear it,
'Tis next my heart; no pow'r shall force it thence,
Whene'er you see it in another's hand
Conclude me dead."—My curses on them both!
How tamely I peruse my shame! But thus,
Thus, let me tear the guilty characters
Which register my infamy. And thus,
Thus wou'd I scatter to the winds of heav'n,
The vile complotters of my foul dishonour.
[*Tears the letter in the utmost agitation.*

Enter EDRIC.

EDRIC.

My lord——

DOUGLAS,
(*In the utmost fury, not seeing Edric.*)
The scarf!

EDRIC.
Lord Douglas.

DOUGLAS.
(*still not hearing him.*)
Yes, the scarf!
Percy, I thank thee for the glorious thought!
I'll cherish it; 'twill sweeten all my pangs,
And add a higher relish to revenge!

EDRIC.

EDRIC.

My lord!

DOUGLAS.

How, Edric here?

EDRIC.

What new distress?

DOUGLAS.

Dost thou expect I shou'd recount my shame?
Dwell on each circumstance of my disgrace,
And swell my infamy into a tale?
Rage will not let me—But—my wife is false.

EDRIC.

Art thou convin'd?

DOUGLAS.

      The chronicles of hell
Cannot produce a falser.—But what news
Of her curs'd paramour?

EDRIC.

He has escap'd.

DOUGLAS.

Hast thou examin'd ev'ry avenue?
Each spot? The grove? the bower, her fav'rite
  haunt?

EDRIC.

I've search'd them all.

DOUG.

DOUGLAS.

     He shall be yet pursu'd,
Set guards at every gate.—Let none depart,
Or gain admittance here without my knowledge.

EDRIC.

What can their purpose be?

DOUGLAS.

     Is it not clear?
Harcourt has rais'd his arm against my life?
He fail'd; the blow is now reserv'd for Percy;
Then with his sword fresh reeking from my heart,
He'll revel with that wanton o'er my tomb;
Nor will he bring her ought she'll hold so dear,
As the curs'd hand with which he slew her husband.
But he shall die! I'll drown my rage in blood,
Which I will offer as a rich libation,
On thy infernal altar, black Revenge?
          [*Exeunt.*

SCENE *changes to the Garden.*

Enter ELWINA.

ELWINA.

Each avenue is so beset with guards,
And lynx-ey'd Jealousy so broad awake,
He cannot pass unseen. Protect him heav'n!

Enter BIRTHA.

My Birtha, is he safe? Has he escap'd!

Birtha.

I know not. I difpatch'd young Harcourt to him,
To bid him quit the Caftle, as you order'd,
Reftore the fcarf, and never fee you more.
But how the hard injunction was receiv'd,
Or what has happen'd fince, I'm yet to learn.

Elwina.

O when fhall I be eas'd of all my cares,
And in the quiet bofom of the grave
Lay down this weary head? I'm fick at heart!
Shou'd Douglas intercept his flight?

Birtha.

     Be calm;
Douglas this very moment left the Caftle,
With feeming peace.

Elwina.

    Ah, then indeed there's danger!
Birtha, whenc'er Sufpicion feigns to fleep,
'Tis but to make its carelefs prey fecure.

Birtha.

Shou'd Percy once again entreat to fee thee,
'Twere beft admit him; from thy lips alone,
He will fubmit to hear his final doom,
Of everlafting exile.

Elwina.

   Birtha, no:
If honour wou'd allow the wife of Douglas
To meet his rival, yet I durft not do it.
Percy! too much this rebel heart is thine:

Too

Too deeply should I feel each pang I gave;
I cannot hate—but I will banish thee.
Inexorable duty, O forgive,
If I can do no more!

BIRTHA.

If he remains,
As I suspect, within the castle walls,
'Twere best I sought him out.

ELWINA.

Then tell him, Birtha,
But Oh! with gentleness, with mercy tell him,
That we must never, never meet again.
The purport of thy tale must be severe,
But let thy tenderness embalm the wound
My virtue gives. O soften his despair;
But say—we meet no more.

Enter PERCY.

Rash man, he's here!
(*She attempts to go, he seizes her hand.*)

PERCY.

I will be heard; nay, fly not; I will speak;
Lost as I am, I will not be denied
The mournful consolation to complain.

ELWINA.

Percy, I charge thee, leave me.

PERCY.

Tyrant, no:
I blush at my obedience, blush to think
I left thee here alone, to brave the danger
I now return to share.

ELWINA.

That danger's past:
Douglas was soon appeas'd; he nothing knows.
Then leave me, I conjure thee, nor again
Endanger my repose. Yet, e'er thou goest,
Restore the scarf.

PERCY.

Unkind Elwina, never:
'Tis all that's left me of my buried joys,
All, which reminds me that I once was happy.
My letter told thee I wou'd ne'er restore it.

ELWINA.

Letter? what letter?

PERCY.

That I sent by Harcourt.

ELWINA.

I
Which I have ne'er receiv'd. Douglas perhaps—
Who knows?

BIRTHA.

Harcourt, t'elude his watchfulness,
Might prudently retire.

EL-

PERCY.

ELWINA!

Grant heav'n it prove so!
(*Elwina going, Percy holds her.*)

PERCY.

Hear me, Elwina, the most savage honour
Forbids not that poor grace.

ELWINA.

It bids me fly thee.

PERCY.

Then e'er thou go'st, if we indeed must part,
To sooth the horrors of eternal exile,
Say but—thou pity'st me!

ELWINA (*weeps.*)

O Percy—pity thee!
Imperious honour;—surely I may pity him.
Yet, wherefore pity? no, I envy thee:
For thou hast still the liberty to weep,
In thee 'twill be no crime; thy tears are guiltless,
For they infringe no duty, stain no honour,
And blot no vow: but mine are criminal,
Are drops of shame which wash the cheek of guilt,
And every tear I shed dishonours Douglas.

PERCY.

I swear my jealous love e'en grudges thee
Thy sad pre-eminence in wretchedness.

ELWINA.

Rouse, rouse, my slumb'ring virtue! Percy hear
   me.
Heav'n, when it gives such high-wrought souls as
   thine,
Still gives as great occasions to exert them.
If thou wast form'd so noble, great, and gen'rous,
'Twas to surmount the passions which enslave
The gross of humankind—Then think, O think,
She, whom thou once didst love, is now another's.

PERCY.

Go on—and tell me that that other's Douglas.

ELWINA.

Whate'er his name, he claims respect from me:
His honour's in my keeping, and I hold
The trust so pure, its sanctity is hurt,
Ev'n by thy presence.

PERCY.

          Thou again hast conquer'd.
Celestial Virtue, like the angel-spirit,
Whose flaming sword defended Paradise,
Stands guard on ev'ry charm.—Elwina, yes,
To triumph over Douglas, we'll be virtuous.

ELWINA.

'Tis not enough to be,—we must appear so:
Great souls disdain the shadow of offence,
Nor must their whiteness wear the stain of guilt.

                                 PER-

Percy.

I shall retract—I dare not gaze upon thee;
My feeble virtue staggers, and again
The fiends of jealousy torment and haunt me.
They tear my heart strings.——Oh!

Elwina.

      No more;
But spare my injur'd honour the affront
To vindicate itself.

Percy.

    But love!

Elwina.

      But glory!

Percy.

Enough! a ray of thy sublimer spirit,
Has warm'd my dying honour to a flame!
One effort and 'tis done. The world shall say,
When they shall speak of my disastrous love,
Percy deserv'd Elwina though he lost her.
Fond tears blind me not yet! a little longer.
Let my sad eyes a little longer gaze,
And leave their last beams here.

Elwina. *(turns from him.)*
  I do not weep.

Percy.

Not weep? Then why those eyes avoiding mine?
        And

And why that, broken voice? those trembling
    accents?
That sigh which rends my soul?

ELWINA

    No more, no more.

PERCY.

That pang decides it. Come—I'll die at once;
Thou pow'r supreme! take all the length of days,
And all the blessings kept in store for me,
And add to her account.—Yet turn once more,
One little look, one last, short glimpse of day,
And then a long, dark night.—Hold, hold my
    heart,
O break not yet, while I behold her sweetness;
For after this dear, mournful, tender moment,
I shall have nothing more to do with life.

ELWINA.

I do conjure thee go.

PERCY.

    'Tis terrible to nature!
With pangs like these the soul and body part!
And thus, but Oh, with far less agony,
The poor departing wretch still grasps at being,
Thus clings to life, thus dreads the dark unknown,
Thus struggles to the last to keep his hold;
And when the dire convulsive groan of death
Dislodges the sad spirit—thus it stays
And fondly hovers o'er the form it lov'd,
Once, and no more—farewel, farewel!

    EL-

ELWINA.

For ever!
(They look at each other for some time, then
[*Exit Percy.*
After a pause,
'Tis past—the conflict's past! retire my Birtha,
I wou'd address me to the throne of grace.

BIRTHA.
May heav'n restore that peace thy bosom wants?
[*Exit Birtha.*

ELWINA.
(*kneels.*
Look down, thou awful, heart-inspecting judge,
Look down, with mercy, on thy erring creature,
And teach my soul the lowliness it needs!
And if some sad remains of human weakness,
Shou'd sometimes mingle with my best resolves,
O breathe thy spirit on this wayward heart,
And teach me to repent th' intruding sin,
In its first birth of thought!
(*Noise without.*)
What noise is that?
The clash of swords! Shou'd Douglas be return'd?

Enter DOUGLAS *and* PERCY *fighting.*

DOUGLAS.
Yield, villain, yield.

PERCY.
Not till this good right arm
Shall fail its master.

Doug-

DOUGLAS.
This to thy heart then.

PERCY.
Defend thy own.
(They fight. Percy disarms Douglas.)

DOUGLAS.
Confusion, death, and hell!

EDRIC. *(Without*
This way I heard the noise.
(Enter Edric and many Knights and Guards from every part of the Stage.)

PERCY.
Curs'd treachery!
But dearly will I sell my life.

DOUGLAS.
Seize on him.

PERCY.
I'm taken in the toils.
(Percy is surrounded by Guards, who take his sword.

DOUGLAS.
In the curs'd snare
Thou laid'st for me, traytor, thyself art caught.

ELWINA.
He never sought thy life.

DOUGLAS.

Douglas.

　　　　Adultress, peace.
The villain Harcourt too——but he's at rest.

Percy.

Douglas, I'm in thy pow'r, but do not triumph,
Percy's *betray'd*, not *conquer'd*. Come, dispatch me.

Elwina. *(to Douglas.*
O do not, do not kill him!

Percy.
　　　　Madam, forbear;
For by the glorious shades of my great fathers,
Their godlike spirit is not so extinct,
That I should owe my life to that vile Scot.
Tho' dangers close me round on every side,
And death besets me—I am Percy still.

Douglas.

Sorceress, I'll disappoint thee—he shall die;
Thy minion shall expire before thy face,
That I may feast my hatred with your pangs,
And make his dying groans, and thy fond tears,
A banquet for my vengeance.

Elwina.

　　　　Savage tyrant!
I wou'd have fallen a silent sacrifice,
So thou had'st spar'd my fame.—I never wrong'd
　　thee.

Percy.

She knew not of my coming;—I alone,
Have been to blame—Spite of her interdiction,
I hither came. She's pure as spotless saints.
　　　　K　　　　　　　　El-

ELWINA.

I will not be excus'd by Percy's crime;
So white my innocence it does not ask
The shade of others' faults to set it off,
Nor shall he need to sully his fair fame,
To throw a brighter lustre round my virtue.

DOUGLAS.

Yet he can only die—but death for honour!
Ye pow'rs of hell, who take malignant joy,
In human bloodshed, give me some dire means,
Wild as my hate, and desperate as my wrongs!

PERCY.

Enough of words. Thou know'st I hate thee,
    Douglas;
'Tis stedfast, fix'd, hereditary hate,
As thine for me; our fathers did bequeath it,
As part of our unalienable birthright,
Which nought but death can end.—Come, end it
    here.

ELWINA. *(kneels.)*

Hold, Douglas, hold!—not for myself I kneel,
I do not plead for Percy, but for thee:
Arm not thy hand against thy future peace,
Spare thy brave breast the tortures of remorse,—
Stain not a life of unpolluted honour,
For oh! as surely as thou strik'st at Percy,
Thou wilt for ever stab the fame of Douglas.

PERCY.

Finish the bloody work.

DOUGLAS.

DOUGLAS.
      Then take thy wish.

PERCY.
Why dost thou start?
    Percy bares his bosom, Douglas advances to stab him, and discovers the Scarf.

DOUGLAS.
          Her scarf upon his breast!
The blasting sight converts me into stone,
Withers my powers like cowardice, or age,
Curdles the blood within my shiv'ring veins,
And palsies my bold arm.

PERCY. *(ironically to the Knights)*
          Hear you, his friends!
Bear witness to the glorious, great exploit,
Record it in the annals of his race,
That Douglas the renown'd—the valiant Douglas,
Fenc'd round with guards, and safe in his own
      castle,
Surpris'd a knight unarm'd, and bravely slew him.

DOUGLAS. *(throwing away his dagger.*
'Tis true—I am the very stain of knighthood.
How is my glory dimm'd!

ELWINA.
          It blazes brighter!
Douglas was only brave—he now is gen'rous!

PERCY.

Percy.

This action has restor'd thee to thy rank,
And makes thee worthy to contend with Percy.

Douglas.

Thy joy will be as short as 'tis insulting.
                            (to Elwina)
And thou, imperious boy, restrain thy boasting.
Thou hast sav'd my honour, not remov'd my hate,
For my soul loaths thee for the obligation.
Give him his sword.

Percy.

        Now thou'rt a noble foe,
And in the field of honour I will meet thee,
As knight encountring knight.

Elwina.

        Stay, Percy, stay,
Strike at the wretched cause of all, strike here,
Here sheathe thy thirsty sword, but spare my
     husband.

Douglas.

' Turn, Madam, and address those vows to me,
To spare the precious life of him you love.
Ev'n now you triumph in the death of Douglas,
Now your loose fancy kindles at the thought,
And wildly rioting in lawless hope,
Indulges the adultery of the mind.
But I'll defeat that wish—Guards bear her in.
Nay, do not struggle.   *(She is borne in.*

Percy.

PERCY.
    Let our deaths suffice,
And rev'rence virtue in that form infhrin'd.

DOUGLAS.
  Provoke my rage no farther.—I have kindled
The burning torch of never-dying vengeance
At Love's expiring lamp.—But mark me, friends,
If Percy's happier genius fhou'd prevail,
And I fhou'd fall, give him safe conduct hence,
Be all obfervance paid him.—Go, I follow thee.
                      (Afide to Edric.
Within I've fomething for thy private ear.

PERCY.
  Now fhall this mutual fury be appeas'd!
Thefe eager hands fhall foon be drench'd in
    flaughter!
Yes—like two famifh'd vultures fnuffing blood,
And panting to deftroy, we'll rufh to combat;
Yet I've the deepeft, deadlieft caufe of hate,
I am but Percy, thou'rt—Elwina's hufband.

End of the Fourth Act.

ACT V.

SCENE, *Elwina's Apartment.*

ELWINA.

THOU who in judgment still remember'st mercy,
Look down upon my woes, preserve my husband.
Pre'erve my husband! Ah, I dare not ask it;
My very pray'rs may pull down ruin on me!
If Douglas shou'd survive, what then becomes
Of—him—I dare not name? And if he conquers
I've slain my husband. Agonizing state!
When I can neither hope, nor think, nor pray,
But guilt involves me. Sure to know the worst,
Cannot exceed the torture of suspense,
When each event is big with equal horror,
(Looks out.
What no one yet? This solitude is dreadful!
My horrors multiply!

Enter BIRTHA.
Thou messenger of woe!

BIRTHA.

Of woe indeed!

EL-

ELWINA.
How, is my husband dead?
Oh speak.

BIRTHA.
Your husband lives.

ELWINA.
Then farewel Percy!
He was the tenderest, truest!—Bless him heav'n,
With crowns of glory, and immortal joys!

BIRTHA.
Still are you wrong; the combat is not over.
Stay, flowing tears, and give me leave to speak.

ELWINA.
Thou say'st that Percy and my husband live:
Then why this sorrow?

BIRTHA.
What a task is mine?

ELWINA.
Thou talk'st as if I were a child in grief,
And scarce acquainted with calamity.
Speak out, unfold thy tale whate'er it be,
For I am so familiar with affliction,
It cannot come in any shape will shock me.

BIRTHA.
How shall I speak? Thy husband——

ELWINA.
What of Douglas?

BIR-

BIRTHA.

When all was ready for the fatal combat,
He call'd his chosen knights, then drew his sword,
And on it made them swear a solemn oath,
Confirm'd by ev'ry rite religion bids,
That they wou'd see perform'd his last request,
Be it whate'er it wou'd.   Alas! they swore.

ELWINA.

What did the dreadful preparation mean?

BIRTHA.

Then to their hands he gave a poison'd cup,
Compounded of the deadliest herbs, and drugs;
Take this, said he, it is a husband's legacy;
Percy may conquer—and—I have a wife!
If Douglas falls, Elwina must not live.

ELWINA.

Spirit of Herod! Why 'twas greatly thought!
'Twas worthy of the bosom which conceiv'd it!
Yet 'twas too merciful to be his own.
Yes, Douglas, yes, my husband, I'll obey thee,
And bless thy genius which has found the means
To reconcile thy vengeance with my peace,
The deadly means to make obedience pleasant.

BIRTHA.

O spare, for pity spare my bleeding heart!
Inhuman to the last. Unnatural! poison!

ELWINA.

My gentle friend, what is there in a name?
The means are little where the end is kind.
If it disturb thee do not call it poison;
Call it the sweet oblivion of my cares,
My balm of woe, my cordial of affliction,

The

PERCY.

The drop of mercy to my fainting foul,
My kind difmiffion from a world of forrow,
My cup of blifs, my paffport to the fkies.

BIRTHA.
Hark! what alarm is that?

ELWINA.
The combat's over!

Birtha goes out.
(*Elwina ftands in a fix'd attitude, her hands clafp'd.*
Now gracious heav'n fuftain me in the trial,
And bow my fpirit to thy great decrees!

Re-enter BIRTHA.
(*Elwina looks ftedfaftly at her without fpeaking.*

BIRTHA.
Douglas is fall'n.

ELWINA.
Bring me the poifon.

BIRTHA.
Never.

ELWINA.
Where are the knights? I fummon you—approach!
Draw near ye awful minifters of fate,
Dire inftruments of pofthumous revenge!
Come—I am ready, but your tardy juftice
Defrauds the injur'd dead.—Go, hafte, my friend,
See that the caftle be fecurely guarded,
Let ev'ry gate be barr'd—prevent his entrance.

L   BIRTHA.

BIRTHA.
Whose entrance?

ELWINA.
His—the murderer of my husband.

BIRTHA.
He's single, we have hosts of friends.

ELWINA.
No matter;
Who knows what love and madness may attempt?
But here I swear by all that binds thee good,
Never to see him more.—Unhappy Douglas!
O if thy troubled spirit still is conscious
Of our past woes, look down and hear me swear,
That, when the legacy thy rage bequeathed me,
Works at my heart and conquers struggling nature,
Ev'n in that agony I'll still be faithful.
She who cou'd never love, shall yet obey thee,
Weep thy hard fate, and die to prove her truth.

BIRTHA.
O unexampled virtue!
                    (a noise without.

ELWINA.
Heard you nothing?
By all my fears th' insulting conqueror comes.
O save me, shield me!

Enter DOUGLAS.
        Heav'n and earth, my husband!

DOUGLAS.
Yes—
To blast thee with the sight of him, thou hast

Of him thou haſt wrong'd, Adultereſs, 'tis thy
    huſband.

           ELWINA *(kneels.)*
Bleſt be the fountain of eternal mercy,
This load of guilt is ſpar'd me! Douglas lives!
Perhaps both live! *(to Birtha)* Cou'd I be ſure of
    that,
The poiſon were ſuperfluous, joy wou'd kill me.

           DOUGLAS.
Be honeſt now, for once, and curſe thy ſtars;
Curſe thy deteſted fate which brings thee back
A hated huſband, when thy guilty ſoul
Revell'd in fond, imaginary joys
With my too happy rival; when thou flew'ſt,
To gratify, impatient, boundleſs paſſion,
And join adulterous luſt to bloody murder;
Then to reverſe the ſcene! polluted woman!
Mine is the tranſport now, and thine the pang.

           ELWINA.
Whence ſprung the falſe report that thou had'ſt
    fall'n?

           DOUGLAS.
To give thy guilty breaſt a deeper wound,
To add a deadlier ſting to diſappointment,
I rais'd it—I contriv'd—I ſent it thee.

           ELWINA.
Thou ſeeſt me bold but bold in conſcious virtue,
—That my ſad ſoul may not be ſtain'd with blood,
That I may ſpend my few ſhort hours in peace,
And die in holy hope of heav'n's forgiveneſs,
Relieve the terrors of my lab'ring breaſt,
Say I am clear of murder—ſay he lives,
Say but that little word that Percy lives,

And Alps, and Oceans shall divide us ever,
As far as universal space can part us.

DOUGLAS.
Canst thou renounce him?

ELWINA
Tell me that he lives,
And thou shalt be the ruler of my fate,
For ever hide me in a convent's gloom,
From cheerful day-light, and the haunts of men,
Where sad austerity, and ceaseless pray'r,
Shall share my uncomplaining day between them.

DOUGLAS.
O hypocrite! now vengeance to thy office.
I had forgot—Percy commends him to thee,
And by my hand——

ELWINA.
How—by thy hand?

DOUGLAS.
Has sent thee,
This precious pledge of love.
(He gives her Percy's Scarf.)

ELWINA.
Then Percy's dead!

DOUGLAS.
He is.—O great revenge, thou now art mine!
See how convulsive sorrow rends her frame!
This, this is transport!—injur'd honour, now,
Receives its vast, its ample retribution.
She sheds no tears, her grief's too highly wrought;
'Tis

'Tis speechless agony.—She must not faint—
She shall not 'scape her portion of the pain.
No! she shall feel the fulness of distress,
And wake to keen perception of her loss.

BIRTHA.

Monster! Barbarian! leave her to her sorrows.

ELWINA. *(In a low broken voice.)*

Douglas—think not I faint, because thou see'st
The pale and bloodless cheek of wan despair.
Fail me not yet, my spirits; thou cold heart,
Cherish thy freezing current one short moment,
And bear thy mighty load a little longer.

DOUGLAS.

Percy, I must avow it, bravely fought,—
Died as a hero shou'd;—but, as he fell,
Hear it, fond wanton, call'd upon thy name,
And his last guilty breath sigh'd out—Elwina!
Come—give a loose to rage, and feed my soul
With wild complaints, and womanish upbraidings.

ELWINA. *(In a low solemn voice.)*

No:
The sorrow's weak that wastes itself in words,
Mine is substantial anguish—deep, not loud;
I do not rave.——Resentment's the return
Of common souls for common injuries.
Light grief is proud of state, and courts compassion;
But there's a dignity in cureless sorrow,
A sullen grandeur which disdains complaint.
Rage is for little wrongs—Despair is dumb.
          [*Exeunt Elwina and Birtha.*

DOUGLAS.

Why this is well!—her sense of woe is strong!
The sharp, keen tooth of gnawing Grief devours
 her,—
Feeds on her heart, and pays me back my pangs,
Since I must perish, 'twill be glorious ruin :
I fall not singly, but, like some proud tower,
I'll crush surrounding objects in the wreck,
And make the devastation wide and dreadful.

Enter RABY.

RABY.

O whither shall a wretched father turn ?
Where fly for comfort ? Douglas, art thou here ?
I do not ask for comfort at thy hands,
I'd but one little casket, where I lodg'd
My precious hoard of wealth, and, like an ideot,
I gave my treasure to another's keeping,
Who threw away the gem, nor knew its value,
But left the plunder'd owner quite a beggar.

DOUGLAS.

What ! art thou come to see thy race dishonour'd ?
And thy bright sun of glory set in blood ?
I wou'd have spar'd thy virtues, and thy age,
The knowledge of her infamy.

RABY.

'Tis false.
Had she been base, this sword had drank her blood.

DOUGLAS.

Ha ! dost thou vindicate the wanton ?

RABY.

RABY.

                    Wanton?
Thou hast defam'd a noble lady's honour—
My spotless child—in me behold her champion:
The strength of Hercules will nerve this arm,
When lifted in defence of innocence.
The daughter's virtue for the father's shield,
Will make old Raby still invincible.
                              (*Offers to draw*.

DOUGLAS.

Forbear.

RABY.

        Thou dost disdain my feeble arm,
And scorn my age.

DOUGLAS.

            There will be blood enough;
Nor need thy wither'd veins, old lord, be drain'd,
To swell the copious stream.

RABY.

    Thou wilt not kill her?

DOUGLAS.

Oh, 'tis a day of horror!

Enter EDRIC *and* BIRTHA.

EDRIC.

            Where is Douglas?
I come to save him from the deadliest crime
Revenge did ever meditate.

DOUGLAS.

                What mean'st thou?
                            EDRIC.

PERCY.

EDRIC.
This inſtant fly, and ſave thy guiltleſs wife.

DOUGLAS.
Save that perfidious——?

EDRIC.
That much injur'd woman.

BIRTHA.
Unfortunate indeed, but O moſt innocent!

EDRIC.
In the laſt ſolemn article of death,
That truth-compelling ſtate, when ev'n bad men
Fear to ſpeak falſly, Percy clear'd her fame.

DOUGLAS.
I heard him—'Twas the guilty fraud of love.
The ſcarf, the ſcarf! that proof of mutual paſſion,
Giv'n but this day, to ratify their crimes!

BIRTHA.
What means my lord? This day? that fatal ſcarf
Was giv'n long ſince, a toy of childiſh friendſhip;
Long e'er your marriage, e'er you knew Elwina.

RABY.
'Tis I am guilty.

DOUGLAS.
Ha!

RABY.
I,—I alone.
Confuſion, honour, pride, parental fondneſs

Distract my soul.——Percy was not to blame,
He was—the destin'd husband of Elwina!
He lov'd her—was belov'd,—and I approv'd.
The tale is long.——I chang'd my purpose since,
Forbad their marriage.

DOUGLAS.

And confirm'd my mis'ry!
Twice did they meet to day—my wife and Percy.

RABY.

I know it.

DOUGLAS.

Ha! thou knew'st of my dishonour?
Thou was a witness, an approving witness,
At least a tame one!

RABY.

Percy came, 'tis true,
A constant, tender, but a guiltless lover.

DOUGLAS.

I shall grow mad indeed! a guiltless lover!
Percy, the guiltless lover of my wife!

RABY.

He knew not she was married.

DOUGLAS.

How? is't possible?

RABY.

Douglas, 'tis true; both, both were innocent:
He, of her marriage, she, of his return.

BIRTHA.

But now, when we believ'd thee dead, she vow'd

Never

O thou Eternal! take him to thy mercy,
Nor let this sin be on his head, or mine!

RABY.

I have undone you all—the crime is mine!
O thou poor injur'd saint, forgive thy father,
He kneels to his wrong'd child.

ELWINA.

     Now you are cruel.
Come near, my father, nearer—I wou'd see you.
But mists and darkness cloud my failing sight.
O Death! suspend thy rights for one short moment,
'Till I have ta'en a father's last embrace—
A father's blessing.—Once—and now 'tis over.
Receive me to thy mercy—gracious heaven.
She dies.

RABY.

She's gone! for ever gone! Cold, dead and cold.
Am I a father? Fathers love their children——
I murder mine! With impious pride I snatch'd
The bolt of vengeance from the hand of heav'n.
My punishment is great—but Oh! 'tis just.
My soul submissive bows. A righteous God
Has made my crime become my chastisement!

End of the Fifth Act.

Lately Published by the same AUTHOR.

1. SACRED DRAMAS; chiefly intended for Young Persons; the Subjects taken from the Bible.—Fourth Edition. Price 4s. in boards.

2. ESSAYS on VARIOUS SUBJECTS, principally designed for Young Ladies. Price 3s. sewed.

3. FATAL FALSHOOD, a Tragedy. Second Edition. Price 1s. 6d.

4. SIR ELDRED of the BOWER, and THE BLEEDING ROCK, Legendary Tales. A New Edition. Price 1s. 6d.

5. The SEARCH after HAPPINESS, A Pastoral Drama. The Seventh Edition. Price 1s. 6d.

6. An ODE to DRAGON.

7. The INFLEXIBLE CAPTIVE, a Tragedy. The Third Edition.

8. FLORIO, A Tale for **Fine** Gentlemen and Fine Ladies. Second Edition.

Printed for T. CADELL, in the Strand.

www.ingramcontent.com/pod-product-compliance
Lightning Source LLC
Chambersburg PA
CBHW020300090426
42735CB00009B/1158